© 2019 Liz Lampman

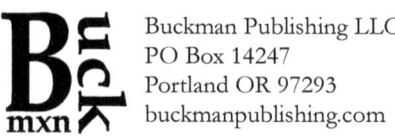

Buckman Publishing LLC
PO Box 14247
Portland OR 97293
buckmanpublishing.com

Another Fortune & Other Poems/Liz Lampman

ISBN: 978-1-7337245-9-3
Library of Congress Control Number: 2019944730

Book design by Megan Sela
Art by Lettie Jane Rennekamp © 2019

Greetings from Portland, Oregon

Another Fortune
&
Other Poems

by
Liz Lampman

FOR SPECK

— you made this livable.

CONTENTS

LITTLE TO SAY

How did we get here, cheek-kissing
in fitted gowns, the country club aglow?

I cannot count the old dogs
we've put to rest in Arkansan soil,

Wisconsin ash—their passing, our passage
out of childhood. Cannot number the undoings

still haunting our twenties. To say nothing
of the miles we traveled to get here,

you from frozen rivers, I from my Western republic,
to crease our wet eyes and slosh wine

over new appreciations—
a pair of dimples, your fostered cat.

The day to day of adulthood, distilled;
I embellish my malaise and leave out binges

where I'd drink fast just so the hangover's
gritty fangs would nick my sloth nerves.

None of that. Tonight we lick the glaze
of our accumulated sisterhood:

postcards, songs from your cello,
memories of our walk through the French Quarter

in spring—piercing our ears and luring
buskers from Jackson Square

—eating each other up like beignets
at midnight. See? The midwest piles up in us

like a hill of moths, and this wedding,
a funeral for youth. With your cheeks lucent

under the chatter of a chandelier, the carpet
soaked with booze, and the reception almost

over, I choke on another dawn:
if not for this reunion, I'd have foregone

this unsparing wedding as
there's little to say of such decadence.

DRINK

See, this porch has had its share
of everything. Its wood, though
warped and disrepaired, never

drinks. Not rye or absinthe puddled
sickly on the boards—no, the sazerac's
candy burn fails to impress this

sagging terrace smoldering on as coal
beneath the eaves. Although my foot
glances toward his thigh and his hand

presses on my forearm, our company
is obsolete. This portico—content
with former carnage dusted

and caked to its planks—and the adirondack
chairs, free of lust, counsel us
with a deep recline that slumbers toward

tomorrow. Still our flesh is deaf,
and with each manhattan our niceties
crumble to the red earth, coy postures

seep toward further mixing.
With bourbon's glaze his eyes undo me
blink by blink, his chin joins my thigh,

slivers of chipped paint become my hair.
We pour the sweetened liquor on our skin,
believe our bodies will never dry.

COME ON

I climb you like a money jug.
Cling to your flesh rungs
with grip and maw. Swallow
the gap between not knowing you
and knowing you. I (marauder
of surrender's hiss) slip up
your sweat-wet chest, press you
back against the sink. Now, dig
into my hips. Lift me and I feed
your heat. Have you come
prepared for the opening? I'm like
triton, handsaw, or shears, aimed
at the body's torrid vice. Don't
pause while I'm propped here
between fridge and counter
yielding to your beat.
Hold the phone, you say
—I'm panting—take a drink
before resuming. Faucet running,
the oven hot—come on,
while we're drunk on it! Each others'
strangeness, the linden trees' brief
blossoms, our tandem percussion
shaking the whole apartment floor.

ANOTHER FORTUNE

We're skipping high above river and rails,
racing trains heading north—perch at the bluff
and peer West at the hills' sun-shimmering shawl!

All summer we kiss lush bloom by rickey,
collins—pour! Mules for you, gin fizz for me!
Alt by ale by bitter by pale, we folly

on. And on and on we whir across the city
giddy as freckles, as fawn. Skin to skin,
so we began, so we are tonight: grown

children in an empty park pumping back
and forth the eager swings. Agents of lust,
we gulp the city's flavored creams until

our eyes are glazed with milk-drunk dreams. Better to
blush than stay sober, here our drunk parade!

Youth's rush never over—here our drunk charade:
get lit with spliffs, race by bike, catch the crew
at Yur's, Portland's finest smoke-drenched dive, then
devour! A heavy table: liver mousse,
ham hock, fois gras, charred delicata squash,
radicchio, grass-fed steak tartare—ah!
Give me digestifs: amaro, fernet
branca, angostura, pehchaud's, coca
cola… Dear Mecca for flesh-eaters, food
mag readers, sugar-spun, purple haze Rose
City, how could the satisfaction last?
Tomorrow, I go, leave such buzz. Work
beckons, demands, touts "opportunity."
To southern plains. I go, chin up, no sighs.

But in Oklahoma, love, the wind shakes me dry.
Imagine all my wetness beading up
into a harvest on my skin, then
whipping away by sky's rusty slap like
the pecans fall here—no ceremony
to their gravity, no grace. Each nutshell
bombs the clay below with a blackstripe dive,
lodges narrow end in the unraked yard
—a sea of rotting meat, or, feast for strays.
The crop goes to waste, my devotion grows
fetid, while over the phone, we manage
elaborate vows: plans to integrate
our books and LPs. Speak of our bodies
like berries wet with rain, teeming with thorns.

Like berries wet with rain, teeming, horny,
we ripen in time for brief reunion.

While apart, talk of kink kept us virile,
but with no cell between us when we meet,
my body shies and binds. Though I never forget

how to take you into my mouth, how to
wind myself around you, the intrusions
into flesh, wet hollows, and vesseled walls
—the intrusions of sex feel foreign,

a stretch I can barely bear. Alone I was
sower and reaper, lord of loam, combing
oxide from clay in this red hell. Now, am I

migrant or doll? All curled locks and budcolored
lips, or laborer with rotting loot?

Lips locked, I labor, lugging rotting fruit
    and roller bag back and forth across this
        manifold land. Racing from place to place
    like, *when I get home I'll feel again, when*
I get out I'll be myself. Again. In
    aluminum and steel I reel from single
        to double bed, plagued by leaden body,
    sad, swollen head. When en route to Tulsa
I avoid the turnpike bridge, her guardrails
    daring me to test their brawn. So I mourn
        first truant joy, then sudden death—dear friend
    pitched from road trip nap into permanent
night—no reason keeps me on the road, just
    inertia and my shepherd's sleeping sighs.

When frost shepherds out harvest, winter pries
warmth from bone, so you keep vinyl spinning,
soothing static in your lamp lit home. Then
I visit your pocket in the city,
snug above Swan Island where the trains yawn
in the Willamette's cradle, to see you.

I've flown across the country with nothing
on my tongue. I open the window, drink
the highway's belching sighs; lie on your bed
and let memory haunt until I belong again.

You come home from Happy House with white boxes
of sweet and sour pork, fried rice, soy sauce,
folded cookies with lips blooming paper.
One reads, *What about another fortune?*

And yet I dream about another fortune:
a boot-clad musician penning lyrics
on my eyes; sharp-tempered poet with tears
for good craft; cigarette-lighting Texan;
rock climber; bike fixer; filigree coated
prophet with rotted core… sometimes I peer
at each woman/man/non-bi, like, will you
be mine? Some obsession with possibility
of more and more potent chemistry. Or
someone to simply challenge me? Hardened,
I wait for one to crack the quenched ego
in my chest. Undress me first, then I'll get
naked. Or, is the answer closer at hand?
(J and I keep pace along the river,
our dogs heeling like sidecars.)
So young when we met that I put stock in
yellow dresses, vintage styles, bold-cut bangs.
Said "artist" with flair and blamed my mother
for every trouble. Most of all, before
my lesbian tongue knew its name. And you
know the woman I want—my warm skin when
she nears—no secret. No reprieve. Pray
my devotion is a slow cancer that
attacks the friendship last. Still, is another
woman the answer? Oh woe, poor queer thing,
betrothed too soon—you see my wanting bones,
say, *let in the world*, and we inside-out promise,
seek out coital tonic. But all the roaming
goes to my head and I begin to wonder
whether or not there's a better offer.

Whether or not there's a better offer,
I wonder. Besides, around me others
hover (or so I think) offering cig
and drink after drink—the barback I come
back for every night, seminar friend, officemate.
Cue in hand, I strike the balls askew,
pretend to love the smoky hue, and pose
hips well-cocked to the side, imploring my next
quarry to sidle up behind and steer
wrist with tight angle, a little english,
slide stick and sink solid after solid.
Game after game, until quarters wane then
I'm back to the rail, side-eye incact,
to lure another body back. Each flame
burns hard then dies away, disinterested...

Or afraid to stay. One woman seems interested,
          texts me back. We thumb and flirt,
we're both drawn in. We trade sun signs, then scent,
          then skin, and on her shoulder Shakespeare's ink:
grace, kill me with spites yet we must not be
          foes. So through complication, attraction
grows. I sing her "Dreams," she licks my thighs, twisting,
          tossing sheets aside—breath comes quick as folds
uncrease—undulating as water
          and flame. But this affair would always
be deprived—brief ambrosia frozen by
          space and time (open status is always
partially contrived). Perfume, tears, and wet
          goodbyes. Another dream I'll never sell.

Goodbye unseen others, I speak my farewell
to broad-chested sky. What is it about
these plains, this red land? How like hell it seemed
at first. Summer's steam yanking stench up from
sewer and the silence of Stillwater
Sundays like resin sealing in heartache.
Gawdy Christians, oil money, frat bar
nights. Iceberg salads, fries, over-cooked steaks,
and football, football (sucker punch to the brain)!

And yet a certain hurt took place, a sense
of home—I hesitate. I know you made this
livable, your voice like amulet for ache.
So let our reunion be reverie
and our perfection rudimentary.

Our perfection—rudimentary and
green. I fill a yellow truck, reverse my trek,
and cross the west again. Less prodigy,

more prodigal craving comfort and banal.
The garden, the yard, the incoming mail—
mundane charms spark avarice and then

home becomes a funhouse of conspicuous
ways to consummate our long-awaited
merry day. We wear the rental out, then

more—cluttered garage, half-finished paint jobs,
our crooked books—*tomorrow*, we say. And
besides, the unwatered herbs survive anyway.

And so our dream, life's petty drill, spins
the year, thus our mission, exemplary!

We perfected our kitchen trajectories:
bob and weave between butcher block and stove,
triangulation among faucet, dishrag,
and drawer. Marking time by the cracks
of the next beers, the beat with light pats
on the ass, content in automation.
Discussing seasoning, you offer herbs
and spice, I agree, nod, it all sounds nice,
but we both know I'll have the final say
in flavor, and you'll finish eating first.
This summer, all we have left is tenderness,
rhythm, none of the sweat you used to drink
from my breastbone, no mention of breakfast—
the dishes air dry on the countertop.

The end began here at the countertop:
    I stood shredding kale when you came in, looped
        your arms around my middle, whispered that
    the grill was hot and ready. The zucchini
was washed and quartered, red onion parsed
    the thick neck of my doubt. My silence and
        grip on the knife rigid against your soft
    voice wanting more. Outside the coals smoldered,
already dwindling, nearing white, inside
    the bavette drinking the marinade's last
        salt, the way my hips poured behind me
    into our beginning—the corporeal
tug that never ceased with feeding. A soft
    summer peach bleeds sugar on the wood.

The rotting fig bleeds ants on the wood and
I've spent the last warm day inventing
reasons for the end; I've tired the dog
with a river full of sinking sticks. Don't
speak my name or feed me meat. Hear my voice
mulled down to a simple syrup of coarse
resolve: I'll drink this up, alone. Please
stay inside with Miles Davis crooning blue,
let me swing dusk away with the brassy
mariachi lighting up the block
from the neighbor's backyard. With all its fruit
on the ground, the tree reaches higher toward
a barren season. A little hunger
is all I ask, can't we skip dinner tonight?

We're skipping again above the railyard,

youth's rush never sober—our last charade!

Because in Oklahoma, love, the wind shakes me dry

despite you, ever wet with rain, teeming, horny,

my lips lock in labor, lugging rotting fruit.

When frost shepherds out harvest, winter pries

and still I dream about another fortune.

Whether or not there's a better offer,

I'm afraid to say. One woman seems interested,

but goodbye others, I speak my farewell.

Our perfection seems rudimentary

and we've perfected kitchen trajectories.

Where we began at the countertop

a rotting fig bleeds ants on the wood.

DREAM WITH LETTERS AND THREAD

We recall our letters,
a compendium of "dears,"
feathers, teeth, the winter.

As fine as a small carcass
picked clean. We do not
mention our coital introduction:

your rants on dismantling civilization
spilling into me as you razed my cunt
with sweet and toothless work;

my breath and earnest pollen
wreaking havoc in your chest.
When the dream turned to gray,

we sealed it with a fraternal kiss
and you sewed my bones
to yours—the needle driving up

diving down—an ampersand
built in air. The tug of thread
between my tarsals. *There,*

there's no forgetting, you said,
there's no losing us now.
Our ruin stitched away.

BUSHEL AND WASTE

for the Orlando 49

I've yet to taste a sand plum, bush gem
of this harsh land. If I retrieve one fallen
fruit from the ground, will I find it empty
where something bored the flesh and pit
away, leaving a hollow tomb? Somehow

these tiny globes hold shapes that grow
less familiar—roundnesses like hope or
an embrace. Will anyone pluck
the apples from the spindling tree in the
vacant lot; its branches droop like wrists

in grief. The waste that coats this earth: mealy
fruit, tattered brown skin, empty shells, and
gunned blood that makes sticky
the steaming cement in front of the club.
Is America an orchard or a rotting promise?

I want to know who holds the bushel;
what profit does massacre yield. How long
until I become a monster too. When
will the spent flesh at our feet
begin to bear something fertile.

RETROSPECTIVE ON WINTER DURING WINTER

am I a radiant lunatic?
— Georgia O'Keeffe

What outerspace is this?
Small boys chase me,
their tennis shoes pounding
the cement-like sky, and I run
through dull fluorescence.
Their curses, biblical chants
imprint on my wax heart.
I have no voice—cannot
summon reason or cast off
their righteous pitch.
All sorts of departure pepper
psyche. Always something
to flee. But what is the point
of escape? Between my ears
a circus of weapons;
behind my eyes a pressing wish
to dissolve into the sea.
Within my lungs, the lunacy
is dancing, and in my hands
the human hair of someone
I should love. What being
is god enough to save me
from myself. From somewhere
else, a prism's faceted light
cracks the question into color.

GOLDRUSH

I found him last spring, holding up
the sagging vegas of an old adobe

portico. His dark and deep-cut eyes leapt
at my form, and he was quick

to gauge my pulse by hand.
I thought him a tonic for the dry

world, but I couldn't see his creeds
propped against the sinking clay. I asked

*is a fly's path more pure clockwise or
counter,* and he smiled like an escaped

prophet, drilled a spile into his veins.
The thin sap pooled, and he and boiled it

parable by parable. Within me
the taste for sweet promise—I drank

his testimony while, across the Pueblo
the Sangres bled their last melt

through the valley where we knelt.
Then what of dust? I asked, *since the neck*

is an extension of the breast? And so,
body to body, we spoke of grace

between lick and chew. Grace
and how the spirit shudders

when pressed through a sieve of flesh.
He preached of our filth and need

for cleansing; I believed.
When we parted—he for the plains

and I for the magpies—I spent the summer
bathing in sagewater steeped from the spindles

we cut out of the valley's throat.
But my yellow bath bit at my urge

to call anything holy, and without
his counsel keeping me high

I became a godclown suckled on
bitter milk. Of course, summer burnt spring away

and there I was: the clay of lust, the dust
of want. Only then did I know thirst was better

than the syrup of blood. That he was filigree
with rotted core. Now, I am a silver

demon, hardened by earth. So, when the chiles
burn in autumn, frost curls the lamb's ear,

and piñon smoke spills from the horno,
I'll call him to a bed of juniper, and preach:

it's the goldrush of your skin I'm after,
not the gospel lacing your tongue.

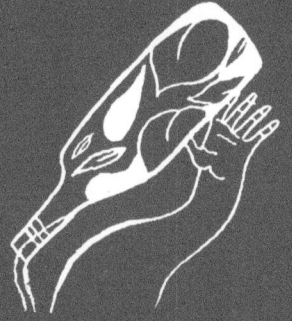

TOEHOLD

All weekend we climbed, our faces lit
from the stones' fractal glow.
I clamored, pink of rebirth in my cheeks,
the bad winter finally forgotten and burning
while you scaled close behind
your body all angles and glue.

The foothills, studded with brick
and hedge, lay below mocking our grins,
my sweat-tracked breasts, the narrow jib
that braced your toehold.
We were better, we thought. Better

than before our bodies met,
traced the Flat Irons' salute, and
painted each other with panting and
laughter. Better, but also scratched,
spent—a little blood beaded up
on your arm. The fucking was becoming
earnest, less wild, less urgent.

Then the cutting loose when we parted,
like feet flailing across a rockface—a scattering
of sparks. Or was it foreclosure? Maybe
this affair had the teeth pulled out of it,
and they chatter between us on the interstate,
prayers at the feet of derricks and bulls.

As I leave, your voice, the mountains
recede into gray; the clouds doubt my progress
the whole drive home. And when I stop for fuel,
what emerges from the slack jaw
of the car door and flies out onto the road
is either a receipt or a note from the future:
Drink only what the mother offers.
So, are you champagne or milk?

Are you the liquid cure for the thirst
that drove me clear across the plains,
I wonder. But there's no coaxing our infant
history to speak. It only babbles.

I think of your body. Where a boulder tore you,
leaving a swath of scarred skin on your scapula,
someone must have mopped your blood.
I want to ask who, but my skin, too, has been host
to many nurses I cannot name. And
what the mother offers?—curiosity full of mud.

What to do with beginning, departing.
With sex and the awkward sound
of your name leaving my face.
What to do with the history of this earth
jutting up into the sky, gazing at us jaggedly.
The asphalt tracks across this grassland
ever leading away and away.

FANTASY, AS A HUNTER

What is a hunter doing at sea?
Daylight comes and goes,

my camouflage is pointless and
I'm thinking about grandeur all the time

—marigold throw pillows and
white marble floors. Parts of this life

come easy (polishing the gun
with finer and finer grit) but

digesting bones, not so. And the prey,
the prey can be very beautiful.

Apollo, Artemis... I'd rather
have them over to dine, than stalk

their shimmering skin. Just think:
all three of us singing

like Judy Garland, in technicolor,
heralding a desert backdrop

for its promise of true love,
and speeding through a valley of wily

sage in the rusted bed of a pick-up
truck. My fantasy: the rifle

becomes sunflower, or spoon, or
an old wooden bat cut down

to fit a child's swing. And all the old lovers
forgotten like sand castles

gently dismantled by a risen
tide, instead of wiggling around

in my bloodstream like bottom-feeders
or saplings tying roots to my joints. But,

no fantasy. The god-hunter is sailing
over sea with a handful of steel.

ACKNOWLEDGMENTS

With much gratitude from the poet, poems in this collection have appeared in the following publications: *Lunch Ticket - Amuse Bouche:* Drink (previously Longing, as Dirge); *Gulf Stream Lit Mag:* Little to Say; *Buckman Journal 002:* Bushel and Waste, Retrospective on Winter during Winter, Goldrush, Toehold, Fantasy, as a Hunter.

GRATITUDE

Many, many thanks to Rich Perin for your belief in my work, and to Buckman Publishing for allowing me to be here at the beginning of this community and press.

Immense gratitude to the poets and teachers who have directly supported the development of this chapbook: Lisa Lewis, Zachary Schomburg, Janine Joseph, Trey Moody, Timothy Otte, Arlo Voorhees, and Kate Click Williams.

Thanks to Jennifer Kwon Dobbs, David Biespiel, Wendy Willis, Sarah Beth Childers, and Kevin Young—for asking me questions I could not yet answer.

And to all of the above writers (again) as well as Emma Murray, Kate Strum, Melissa Cundieff, Sean Fleming, Clara Swanson, Susannah Clark, and Lettie Jane Rennekamp— thank you for holding space for craft and creation.

Special thanks to Melissa Cundieff and Bryan Borland for your support—you inspire me more than you know.

And to my partner and family who have always known I was capable. I love you so.

Photo by Erika Unyatinski

Liz Lampman holds an MFA in poetry from Oklahoma State University. She received the Edwin Markham Prize for Poetry from Reed Magazine in 2016; her poems have been published by Rattle, Lunch Ticket, The Missing Slate, Gulf Stream Lit Mag, and Timberline Review. Raised in the St. Croix River Valley, she now lives in Portland, Oregon where she teaches creative writing workshops at the Attic Institute and adventures with her dog, Bishop.

Lettie Jane Rennekamp is an illustrator in Portland, Oregon by way of Kentucky. Her illustrations are bold and tender at the same time, depicting motherhood, varying versions of gender expression, community, and nature all together. Her favorite things are swimming in cold water in the summer and soaking in hot water in the winter.